Sales on Rails

A Sales Engineer's Framework for Better Selling

By

John Haldi

for Martin

told ya' I was listening

Table of Contents

A quick note on terminology

For the sake of clarity, I'd like to define a few terms so that we're all on the same page semantically. This book generally is about encounters between buyers and sellers, but it makes sense to be more precise.

I use the term "SE" as short-hand for Sales Engineer. In other companies this role might be called a Solution Consultant (shortened to "SC"), a Pre-sales Engineer, or other names. What I mean by SE is the technical half of a two-person (a.k.a. "four legged") sales team, where the sales person brings along a "techie" to the meeting.

Conversely, I use the term "AE" as short-hand for Account Executive, also known by other terms. When I refer to the AE I'm talking about the other half of a four-legged sales team — the sales rep. The AE is typically focused on the commercial aspects of a transaction — the price, the contract, etc.

When I refer to "solution," I'm using the term generically to mean either a product, service, or some combination of the two. Nothing in this book is specific to selling one or the other, so I settled on the term "solution" as a good catch-all for whatever you happen to be selling. Are there nuances to selling a product as opposed to a service? Sure. But they aren't relevant to the material here.

I also specifically use the term "prospect" rather than "customer," because in my mind a prospect is somebody who is considering a purchase. A customer is somebody who has already bought the solution being offered.

Conversations with customers are very different than conversation with prospects, and in my opinion would fall under the heading of "account management" or "customer service." This book is about sales, so I'm focused on prospects.

That said, there are times when the prospect is already a customer — *i.e.*, you're trying to sell something new to an existing customer. In such a situation, it is true that the person on the other side of the table is a customer, but more importantly that person is a prospect for a new purchase so the material in this book applies.

Finally, throughout the book you'll see that I sometimes refer to "he" or "she," and I do so interchangeably. The use of one pronoun or the other is not meant in any way to suggest that the roles are or should be gender-specific — the choice of pronoun was made throughout the text solely with an eye towards readability and clarity.

Introduction

As an SE, you will almost certainly have to sit through many sales training programs throughout the course of your career. More than likely they will focus on the role of the AE. It's not surprising when you consider that these programs are generally written and taught by former AEs.

I find it very disappointing that the typical sales training programs tend to ignore the role of the SE. In my experience the SE training typically consists of being asked to memorize a presentation and demonstration script, and then having to "do the preso and demo" in front of management so we can get critiqued. It seems to me that all of this "SE training" is geared to allow somebody in management to check a box that says you were trained. For this we typically spend 2-3 days in a windowless conference room and lose a week in the field — time that could be spent selling. Tragic.

While I do believe that AEs play a critical role in the sales process, I believe that SEs play their own distinct role which — when done correctly — can have an even greater impact on sales results than the work done by an AE.

This short book is a clear, simple framework to help SEs make more money and to really enjoy their job. I've captured here what I believe are key principles, strategies and tactics related to doing the job of an SE, and doing it well on a consistent basis.

In the pages that follow you will find my thoughts and opinions about being an SE — what works, what doesn't work, and why. These are based on personal experience working for many years as an SE for several different companies. My opinions are also guided by an earlier time in my career as a purchaser of technology solutions. Not only have I been on a lot of sales calls as an SE, but I've also been the prospect many, many times and been witness to how a lot of AE/SE teams handle their sales calls. (Generally, it ain't pretty.)

Unlike many sales training books, this one is not going to suggest that you put in more hours or do more work. The premise of this book is that the least enjoyable parts of being an SE are also the least effective. Instead of doing 20 things in the hope that one of them is the right thing to do, you should spend the necessary time listening to the prospect so you can determine which few things are the right thing to do and thus skip the bulk of the things that aren't relevant.

The beginning of the book is more about principles — understanding how sales encounters work and why they work the way they do. If you read those sections and think "duh, of course," move on quickly. But if you find yourself reading those and thinking "no, that's wrong," please take some time with an open mind to try to embrace these principles of how interactions work between buyers and sellers.

As the book progresses I move into strategies and tactics — more hands-on, how-to stuff. I believe it's all intuitive stuff once it's been presented. There's nothing to memorize, no cheat sheets to keep handy, no forced acronyms to remember a "system," and no charts or diagrams or worksheets to track each prospect.

If you're like most SEs I know, you've probably been led to believe that selling is a complicated, mysterious process that we, as technologists, struggle to try to learn. It's actually the opposite.

Selling is a very simple, straightforward process that has been done a very long time — long before the concept of an SE ever came along. We, as technologists, like to think that anything good must be really complicated. That's where we're wrong.

Technology is complicated, but selling is not.

Sales is not a black box

Basic value exchange

Contrary to popular misconceptions, "selling" is not a black box, it is not a mystery, it is not some Jedi-like "force" that you must master. Sales happen according to very simple, very basic rules of give and take.

At the risk of stating the obvious, here is the fundamental diagram of what is happening when a sale occurs:

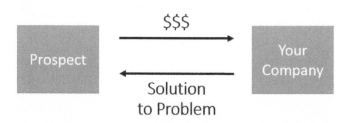

Your prospect has a problem and you have a solution to that problem. Your prospect is willing to exchange money to get a solution to her problem. It's pretty simple stuff.

Now let's add something critical, but not so obvious:

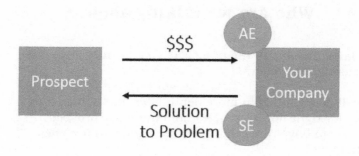

The AE owns the top arrow, the $$$. Anything having to do with price, commercial terms, contracts, etc. is the AE's domain. Stay out of her turf.

The SE owns the bottom arrow, the solution to the problem. Anything having to do with the solution, the technology, the fit with the prospect's problem, etc. is your domain. Your AE should stay out of your turf.

Who are we talking about?

A large number of the prospects you encounter are not potential customers.

We'll discuss this in more depth later, but suffice it to say for right now that at a minimum, your prospect needs to have three things if she is going to become a customer:

1. She needs to have a real problem

2. She needs to know she has a real problem

3. She needs to be motivated to solve her problem

The above three things are properties of the prospect that you cannot change. There are some schools of thought that believe that you can work on #2 and #3, but I disagree. Trying to create awareness of a problem and motivation to solve it is a long, hard slog through the mud, and a money-losing proposition for an SE.

Better to use the above three points as a quick template against which to measure a prospect — and any prospect who fails on any one point should be tossed on the reject pile so you can go look for legitimately qualified prospects.

When we talk here about qualified prospects we're talking about prospects who know they have a real problem and are motivated to solve it.

Information asymmetry

Information asymmetry is that feeling you get when you go to buy something and you know that the salesperson holds all the cards and you hold none. It's the feeling that there's a ton of information that you don't know and the salesperson does, and that information is all stacked against you. If you've ever bought a car or a mattress (to pick a couple of examples), you probably have experienced information asymmetry.

The concept of information asymmetry as it relates to economic transactions (buying and selling) was first studied by an economist named George Akerlof. Back in 1970 he wrote a paper in which he studied the dynamics of the used car market. George struggled to get his paper published because nobody took him seriously — the used car market, really?

But George was onto something. Specifically, he studied what happens in a sales situation when one person (the used car salesman) holds all the cards in terms of information, and the other person (the buyer) holds none of them. He called this "information asymmetry."

In short, it's the fear of buying a lemon.

What George documented in his paper is that information asymmetry causes the buyer to discount the perceived value of the car, regardless of whether the car is a "gem" or a "lemon." In non-technical terms, since everybody thinks the used car salesman is a lying dirt bag, he can't even sell a great car for a decent price because everybody is assuming whatever he says is not true.

Eventually the world noticed that George was onto something with his notion of information asymmetry. In 2001, that paper he could barely get published received the Nobel Prize.

[Random fact: George ended up marrying a lady by the name of Janet Yellen, who is now the head of the Federal Reserve. I'll bet they have smart kids.]

Why AEs need SEs

I share George's story because information asymmetry underpins every sales encounter you will have, and it is why the companies where we work have SEs in the first place (even if our companies seem to have forgotten it).

The reason is because — despite advances in sales training and methodology for AEs — most of the prospects you encounter can't shake that fear of the used car salesman. And it isn't the fault of the AEs. It's simply that when you walk into the room the prospect correctly assumes that when it comes to your solution, you and the AE initially hold all the information cards.

Your prospect doesn't want to buy a lemon and he's afraid you're going to stick him with one. In more concrete terms he is afraid that he's going to hand over a bunch of money in the hopes of solving his problem, and when the dust settles he won't have solved his problem. He doesn't know if you're honest nor whether your solution really does what you say. Just like the used car salesman, your "gem" gets discounted because the prospect thinks "maybe it's a lemon."

Imagine how scary that can be if it is a large ticket item and the prospect isn't 100% convinced that your solution will do what you say. What happens to your prospect if the company spends a million dollars with you and then you don't deliver? Does your prospect lose face with his boss? Does the prospect's company lose customers to competitors? Does their stock go down? More personally, does he not get a bonus this year? Does he get fired? Do other people in his company get laid off?

So, if a prospect is going to spend a large amount of money with your organization he is going to have to trust that you are going to deliver the solution as promised. At some point in the sales process your prospect is going to have to go to his boss and basically say "I've done all the research I can, and I believe that if we go with this proposed solution it will solve the problem." He wants to be sure he's right.

All the above are going through a prospect's mind (consciously and/or subconsciously) as he evaluates you and your solution.

Your AE cannot effectively address the information asymmetry because of her credibility problem. Despite her best efforts, your AE is handicapped by the stereotype of a lying used car salesman.

But an SE can. That's why we're in the room. We don't have that baggage. We're the third party in the room, tasked with being the trusted adviser. Even though we are paid by our company, we can become the credible source of information in the prospect's eyes that balances out the information asymmetry and allows the prospect to overcome the fear of buying.

Discounting value

Now let's go back to our diagram of value exchange and tie it into our friend George's notion of information asymmetry:

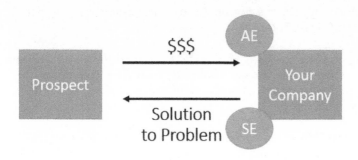

As we've said, the SE owns that bottom arrow. If we don't address that information asymmetry, the prospect is going to discount our gem in her mind by some factor. As the SE, you are in control of how much the prospect is going to discount the value of your solution in her mind.

Your solution might really be worth a $1 million, but if the prospect thinks you're full of crap she might not even think it's worth $100,000. This is before your AE even engages in a conversation about price. This is about the perceived value of the solution in the prospect's mind.

Conversely, if you've done your job and the prospect believes what you've shared and perceives the value of your solution without feeling the need to discount it in her mind, then she too will see it as a $1 million solution.

This is why I believe that the SE is so critical to successful sales. No prospect is going to rationally pay more for a solution than she thinks it's worth. The SE sets the ceiling on what a prospect is willing to pay. If your prospect thinks your solution is only worth $200,000, there's not an AE on the planet who will get her to pay $500,000.

While your role is to make the Perceived Value as BIG as possible in the prospect's mind, your AE's role is to capture as much as possible of the Perceived Value in the Price Paid.

Please pause for a moment and let this model sink in. It is critical for understanding the roles you and your AE play in a properly functioning sales team:

The SE helps the prospect perceive the value of the solution, and the AE tries to capture as much as possible of that perceived value in the price paid.

That's how the best AE/SE teams do it. That's how the pros who consistently go on the Achiever's Club trip every year do it. That's how you take luck out of sales and become selling machines. The AE and the SE both play critical but distinct roles, which when combined properly result in blowing out your quota.

Those of you who have been an SE for some time might already be shaking your head thinking "No, that's not what they teach us." That's because the people who teach you are wrong. It is the reason I wrote this book.

The annual exercise of company sales training invariably focuses on the AE, with only an afterthought given to the SEs. We usually sit through the general presentations and then get shunted to a room to practice the canned PowerPoint and demo. [Sigh.]

Don't let the bad training you've received fool you into thinking that you do not play a critical role in sales achievement.

You can, if you like, accept "the norm" and choose to believe that you just need to give a presentation and a demo and you're done. Your boss might even pat you on the back and consider this acceptable.

But if you want to be a rock-star SE, to blow out your quota, to make more money, to get to go on the annual Achievers Club trip, keep reading.

Key takeaways

- Your AE owns everything to do with commercial terms, you own everything to do with how the solution solves the problem

- A prospect is somebody who knows she has a real problem and wants to try to solve it

- Information asymmetry – the fear of buying a lemon – dominates our sales interactions

- SEs should eliminate that information asymmetry so the prospect can feel comfortable deciding to buy

- SEs determine how much value the prospect perceives in a solution, which ultimately determines the amount paid

AEs

Play your positions

In baseball, a ground ball is hit to the shortstop who fields the ball and throws it to the first baseman. Both the shortstop and the first baseman are critical to the play but do different things. If both do their part, the batter is out. If either of them drops the ball, they don't get the out.

In a sales call, you have your role to play and your AE has her role to play. The roles are different. Both are important. Each is dependent on the other.

An AE cannot and should not try to play your role, nor should you try to play hers. Just like the shortstop can't run the ball to first base to tag the runner, you should never be talking about the price of the solution — that's the AE's role. And just like the first baseman cannot run across the infield to field the ball and then run back to first to get the runner out, your AE shouldn't be talking about your solution and how it solves the prospect's problem.

Many AEs are confident. That's good. You want them to be. Many AEs think they have a "selling system" that works for them. That's bad. They don't.

AEs don't have a selling system. You do. Without you, the prospects won't consistently reach the point of: "I see the value here. I want this solution." As an SE, your system is the key to a potential sale. Your system — focusing on the prospect's problem and helping the prospect decide that your solution will solve that problem — is the selling system.

If the shortstop doesn't field the ball and throw it to first, the first baseman doesn't have a play to make.

AEs have a "closing system." Once you have done your work, the AE has the job of saying to the prospect "I'm sorry to have to tell you this, but this solution is expensive. Here's what it's going to cost you." The AE is the toll-taker. The AE must say "I know you want this, but you have to get through me to get it."

AEs have a hard role to play. Good AEs make it look easy, but it isn't. If it was easy they'd all be good AEs. I was a successful AE earlier in my career. I respect the role and the people who do it well. But personally, I prefer the role of the SE. To me, digging into a prospect's problem and trying to see if we can find a solution together is fun and interesting, whereas discussing price and moving a contract through the legal process is boring. But that's a personal preference, not a judgment on the relative values of the two roles.

What I do know, which applies to all SEs, is that if we play our position well it sets up our AEs to close a lot of deals. If we don't do our job well it means our AEs are probably going to struggle to get near a deal. This is why I say with complete certainty that anybody who thinks an SE's role is somehow junior to or less important than an AE's role is flat-out wrong.

Who is the prospect going to trust?

Close your eyes and imagine a fast-talking, slick car salesman.

Whether AEs like it or not, that's the stereotypical image that the prospect has of your AE when he walks into the room. It doesn't matter how consultative he is, it doesn't matter how articulate he is, it doesn't matter how folksy he is, the prospect intuitively believes that the salesperson is going to do and say anything get the sale.

That's ok. The prospect doesn't have to like the AE — the prospect must get past the AE to buy the solution. The AE is the toll-taker. If the prospect makes the decision to buy, the AE is going to be the bearer of bad news — the price. The prospect probably isn't going to like him at that point anyway, so no sense fretting about it.

Close your eyes again. Picture your doctor in your mind's eye. Smart, educated, honest, trying to diagnose the problem and find the solution.

As an SE, you are that doctor and you must be seen by the prospect as that doctor. You are not the sales person. Got it? You are the SE, and your role is that of the doctor. You are in the business of helping customers solve their problems.

As an SE, you should rid yourself of anything that remotely resembles a "sales person." If you've ever felt "sleazy" as an SE, here's your way to fix that. Nothing about what you do as an SE should feel like being a sales person. It makes no sense for you to also act like a salesperson — there's already an AE in the room. Your company cannot afford to send two AEs on the same call, and they shouldn't.

You are the trusted advisor. You are the car buff your friend brings along to the showroom when he wants to buy a new car. You are the person who is going to help the prospect learn everything she needs to know about your solution so she can decide if it's the right thing to solve her problem. You are not selling, you are helping people find a solution to their problem.

Don't worry about getting the sale. Your AE is already worrying about that. Your prospect needs to trust somebody and it isn't going to be the AE.

Be the doctor. Ask questions. Diagnose. Find solutions. Build the trust your prospect is looking for.

Don't get given away

Your AE must believe and represent to the prospect that you are an invaluable resource whose time is precious, and that the AE is "giving something of value" to the prospect by getting some of your time.

The SE is not junior to the AE. The SE is not an AE's support person. If your AE cannot embrace this concept you are dead in the water before you even walk into the room with the prospect.

When an AE doesn't value an SE, the AE says things like this: "This is my SE and he'll do whatever you need..." (implying you're a non-billable resource and the AE has constant access to you...) At this point your AE has thrown away the opportunity to introduce you with a boatload of credibility. Instead of the expert whose time is precious, you're a lackey with nothing better to do than hang around until given a task. You now enter the conversation with zero credibility and no perceived value on the part of the prospect.

You are the specialist your company keeps on staff to help prospects diagnose their problems and find solutions. When your AE tells a prospect "I think we need to bring an SE into this conversation" it should be said in the same way you might tell somebody "Oh I'm friends with a great doctor who might be able to help — let me see if I can get you on her calendar."

Here's how your introduction should sound to the prospect:

"I don't know if what we have is right for you, but I've got somebody I work with who is very good at figuring out if what we have is a good solution to your problem.

If I can get on his calendar, can we spend some time together digging into things?"

Your prospect has a problem and you're the doctor. Your AE is giving your prospect a free consultation with the doctor. That's very valuable to a prospect. And it sets you up with a huge amount of credibility when you walk into the room.

Even though this might require a step down in an AE's ego (your AE is implying that you are more important and harder to get time from), your AE gets something valuable in return: the prospect owes the AE for getting access to "the doctor" — a bargaining chip she can use to extract valuable information in return. For example, "Mr. Prospect, if I'm going to ask for company resources to get some of this SE's time, I need to justify it internally. Can you tell me where you are in the budgeting and decision making process?"

This is why it is critical for your AE to understand the value you bring to the table and to always represent to the prospect that getting you involved is a gift to the prospect.

Fixin' to get ready

AEs who don't understand the proper roles of AEs and SEs often create mountains of unnecessary work for both the AE and the SE.

The root cause of the problem is that the AE mistakenly believes that it is the AE's job to "sell" the solution to the prospect while you just carry the props and do a song and dance number in the show. AEs are setting themselves up for failure when they try to do this. After several of these types of failed experiences with prospects, AEs become fearful of their next interaction. I don't fault them for being afraid — I'd be afraid of interacting with a prospect too if most of those interactions were failures.

It is human nature that when we must do something we don't want to do (for whatever reason, although fear of failure usually tops the list), we look for ways to avoid doing it. The term for this is "procrastination."

We all do it. We've got something we know we need to do but that something seems "hard." So we find lots of other things to do instead, fooling ourselves that if we're "busy" we're not really avoiding the hard stuff. Procrastination is the result of our subconscious creating excuses for us to avoid the hard work we know we need to be doing.

AEs are not immune. AEs live and die by how much they sell, and every encounter with a prospect can be scary because — heaven forbid — the prospect isn't going to buy. That would mean removing them from the pipeline. That would mean lowering their forecast. That would mean their boss is going to ask tough questions on the next weekly meeting.

Procrastinating AEs create busy work for themselves and for their SEs. They develop charts, and lists, and checklists and who knows what, all to delay engaging the prospect in any activity that might potentially disqualify the prospect. They insist on doing all kinds of research about a prospect, their industry, their competitors, etc. before engaging the prospect. They spend countless hours strategizing how a meeting will go before engaging with the prospect.

Worse still, an AE will commit to additional work for you despite all the evidence indicating that the lead isn't qualified. He'll want you to build a custom "Proof of Concept" demo ("POC") to see if it "turns things around." He'll ask you to fill out a hideously long Request for Proposal ("RFP") on the off chance the prospect surprises us with the business. In the face of overwhelming evidence the prospect doesn't think our solution is a fit to his problem, the AE will want to go back and have another meeting to see if they will change their tune.

When you see this type of behavior in your AE, recognize it for what it is — procrastination. Try to help yourself by helping your AE fight these temptations. It might be nice to say "it's ok if my AE wastes his time doing this stuff, it doesn't affect me." But it does. If your AE is wasting his time — or worse, wasting yours — you aren't making as many sales as you could and that costs you money.

It is your job to control the technical process

When a patient goes to the doctor, they're the customer, right? They're paying for her time and expertise.

But does the doctor let the patient run the appointment? Does the doctor let the patient decide what questions she is going to ask or how the examination is going to go? Or does the doctor ask the questions, direct the conversation, examine relevant things, and then explain what she thinks is the problem and make a recommendation?

It is no different for you, the SE. You are the doctor. The process of asking questions, digging into the answers, examining relevant things, directing the conversation, is owned by you. Not your AE. Not your prospect.

Yes, your prospect is an important business person who should be respected. Yes, your prospect will decide on whether to do business with you. Doctors have CEOs for patients all the time. So will you.

But you need to decide if you can help the prospect. And to do that there is a process that you need to establish and explain to the prospect so that the two of you can evaluate properly if your solution will work for the prospect. And since you do this every day with prospects, you should take the lead in controlling that process.

You are the walking knowledge base (or have access to the right people). Not your AE. You. You are the "doctor," helping to diagnose the prospect's problem and helping the prospect understand whether you do or do not have a way to help the prospect.

At some point the prospect needs to know what's involved in owning, installing, and maintaining it, and they need to make sure that it will play nice in their larger technical ecosystem. Sure. That's bits and bytes stuff. You'll share all that information if and when it is appropriate.

If you don't want this process to go off the rails, own this process. It might be as simple as "before I show you the solution, I need to ask you a few questions so that I can be sure to show you the relevant things." Sometimes it means saying "No, we're not going to do that right now because it doesn't make sense."

Don't let somebody else waste your own time: you MUST control this process and say "For me to be able to justify investing this much time and energy fulfilling your request, I'm going to need to better understand whether this is a proper investment in resources. So first we need to do this..."

You need to do this. Your AE should provide air cover here, and hopefully will. But AEs who don't know better won't. Regardless, you need to own this process. If you don't own it, have fun working late on that RFP for a prospect you already know isn't going to buy your solution.

Manage your time like you'd manage your investments

Until your AE absolutely, positively believes 100% in the value of your time, you will always have to struggle against being asked to do time wasting activities that prevent you from maximizing your earnings. I cannot stress this enough — an AE who does not understand your role and thus doesn't value your time is the biggest threat to your paycheck.

Imagine your stockbroker calls you and says he has the next sure-fire, can't-miss investment opportunity of the year. Unless your stockbroker is Warren Buffett, you probably receive your broker's tip with a good bit of wariness.

Your AE calls and says he has a hot prospect. It's a huge opportunity, big meeting with all the right people, biggest deal of the year. And there you go pulling up the travel system to book a ticket without doing any qualifying whatsoever.

Hello? Should you trust your AE more than a stockbroker? (Hint: Most stockbrokers have "Account Executive" as their title.) At a minimum, you should be peppering your AE with questions to make sure that this trip is for a qualified prospect.

Remember something: an AE doesn't have to take money out of his own pocket to pay you. An AE doesn't pay for your travel to meet the prospect. An AE doesn't care if you must spend 60 hours prepping a custom demo for a prospect, or that you spent two days traveling to and from a prospect for a one hour meeting. Your time seemingly costs your AE nothing. To the AE who doesn't understand the value you bring to the table, you are a free resource.

And if you're like most SEs I know, you probably support anywhere from two to four AEs, perhaps even more. So this problem can be multiplied exponentially.

If you want to keep things on the rails, you should insist on a qualifying conversation WITH THE PROSPECT before you get committed to anything like travel, POCs or RFPs. If the prospect cannot convince you that it is worth your time to get on a plane to visit, why would you? You certainly don't want to take an AE's word for it.

(There is of course a special exception to this rule for the occasional prospect in Hawaii or the Caribbean, but I think we're all aware of that exception so no need to cover it here.)

It is your time we're talking about, and hence your paycheck. Why would you let your AE commit your time without any validation on your part that it is time well spent?

It is critical that you educate your AE on how your time equates to money. Your AE must understand that if he is wasting your time on an unqualified prospect, then you aren't investing your time in a qualified deal that might put money in your pocket and your AE's pocket.

What just happened?

As the doctor, you'll be the focal point of the prospect's process of learning everything necessary to make a decision to buy. And you'll know when and how the information asymmetry has been addressed.

When you've done your job correctly, you can answer the question "Why did the prospect buy?" The answer comes easily: "Oh, she had a huge problem with managing the chaos of distributed content creators spread out across the organization, and our workflow and versioning tools were exactly what she needed."

Amusingly, your AE might not know why.

Even my absolute, all-time favorite AE in the world has trouble staying awake while I'm doing my tech thing. He's heard it so many times before. To him, the prospect and I sound like the teacher in the cartoon Peanuts: "wah wah, wah wah wah wah"

Listen the next time an AE gets asked by management what the key to the sale was. You'll hear something like "Oh it was a team effort — the SE did a wonderful job, the professional services were instrumental, product management played a role." It's a safe political answer, true, but it hides the fact that the AE probably doesn't really know why the prospect bought.

That's ok, so long as your AE knows WHEN the prospect bought.

It's when the prospect starts asking different types of questions that signal she has addressed the information asymmetry and believes that your solution is the right one to solve her problem. It sounds like this:

- "So how long will it take to implement?"

- "Can I get professional services to get this thing set up if I need help?"

- And finally, "So how much does this cost?"

You're done when you hear this. The prospect has decided that they want to buy the solution. You've finished that "bottom arrow" in the diagram.

If you need to, nudge your AE awake. It's time for you to shut up. You've fielded the ball and thrown it to first base. Now the AE must catch the ball. It's time to talk price and that's not your role.

Key takeaways

- AEs and SEs have very different roles, and shouldn't try to play each other's role

- Like it or not, AEs are not seen as trustworthy in the prospect's eyes, but SEs can be

- When you allow your AE' to "give you away," don't be surprised when the prospect thinks you are not valuable

- As an SE you want to engage with a prospect as early as possible in order to get down to business

- Don't let somebody else (the prospect or your AE) set the agenda

- If you let somebody else control the agenda, don't be surprised when they waste your time

- You are the person addressing the information asymmetry, so you know best what tipped the scales and when it happened

You

Little things matter

The prospect MUST trust the SE. You are the doctor, the trusted adviser. No trust, no sale.

Trust is a critical component of the decision-making process for the prospect, since buying encompasses a large element of fear for a prospect. The AE is the gatekeeper with the price list, who isn't going to let the prospect have the solution without paying. The prospect doesn't need to "trust" the AE, since a price to be paid is a given.

Generally, you build trust with another person by repeated episodes of doing what you say and saying what you do. Thus we have the saying "trust is built up a teaspoon at a time, and it can be lost entirely in an instant."

You might be lucky, and begin a relationship with a prospect with an initial level of trust. Perhaps your company has a good relationship. Or perhaps the prospect was referred by somebody who told the prospect she can trust you.

As the relationship evolves you will have little moments when you say you will do something. These are your tests in the prospect's eyes. To you they may seem insignificant, but for a prospect they are very important.

If you tell a prospect you will follow-up with some technical documentation before the end of the week, and then you send it as promised, you've built a little bit of trust. When you don't know the answer to a question but you promise to find out, and then you send an email with that answer, you've built a little trust.

When you blow off doing what you've said, you've blown the opportunity to build trust. And any previous instances of building trust might have just been negated.

It may seem silly, but these little things are tremendously important.

You've told the prospect all these wonderful things about your solution, which the prospect needs to believe to be true. The prospect is looking for clues as to your sincerity. But if you blow the one little demonstrable thing you said you'd do — that you would send some additional material by the end of the week perhaps — you've given the prospect reason to worry about you and your credibility.

This isn't hard. It is simply paying attention to the details. It is correlation between what you say and what you do, which is the definition of sincerity. It is the linchpin to SE credibility.

Remember, any loss of credibility on your part lowers the perceived value of the solution in the prospect's mind, which lowers the maximum price the prospect is willing to pay.

Don't try to be the smartest person in the room

Imagine for a moment that you're not feeling well, so you go to the doctor. And the doctor says "what's bothering you?" You start to explain what's going on, but after just a few moments the doctor interrupts and she says "Oh I know exactly what the problem is!"

But you weren't done explaining things. How does that make you feel?

The doctor just screwed up, big time. Because the doctor was showing off. The doctor wanted to "wow" you with her ability to figure things out super fast.

The doctor didn't listen to what you had to say, so you know the doctor is only guessing at what your problem is. Her credibility with you is now shot, right? You've stopped listening at this point? How could she possibly know what the problem is if you haven't told her about the other two symptoms you're having.

You're probably wondering if it's worth telling her about the other symptoms at this point. If her diagnosis stays the same, you don't know if that's because it's correct, or because she doesn't want to lose face by changing her diagnosis in the face of new information. That's not a good situation for a prospect — oops, I mean patient — is it? Time for a new doctor, right?

(As an aside, a 1999 study published in the Journal of the American Medical Association found that doctors listened to a patient's concerns for an average of 23 seconds before interrupting the patient. I suspect that if we try, we SEs can do a whole lot better than the doctors in that study.)

We've all made this same mistake as an SE. We meet somebody for the first time, we're nervous, we want very much to make a good impression, and then it happens. The conversation goes somewhere where we know a little bit about the topic and we can't help ourselves. We get excited because we know a little bit about what they're talking about and we jump in and add our two cents worth.

Oops.

If you really want the prospect to think you're smart, allow the prospect to educate you as much as possible. And when the prospect is done, ask for more education.

Remember that the most valuable thing that you can do in the eyes of your prospect is to listen. Ask questions if you need to. But listen very carefully. And while it might be nice if you've got something to add to the conversation, just wait. Listen. Be patient. You'll have your time to speak soon enough.

Because what the prospect wants — what she really, really wants — is for you to listen to everything she has to say and then to think for a while. Really think. Think about whether you might be able to solve her problem.

The reason this is so important is that your prospect believes that her problem is unique in some way. If the problem was run of the mill, a dime a dozen, just like everybody else's, she would have solved it already. But in her mind, there is something about her problem that makes her believe it is special and she needs a special solution. That's why you've been invited to meet with her.

And if you won't listen when she tries to explain how her problem is special, why would she listen when you try to tell her your solution is special?

You and the prospect are on the same team

You and the prospect are equals working together to solve something. You are on the same team. Figuratively, you and the prospect should be sitting on the same side of the table. The way you conduct yourself will be reflected right back to you by the prospect. So think about what you want to get back from the prospect and give it first.

Your prospect knows his problem better than you. Maybe you did some research on his company before you came to meet. Maybe you have seen similar problems elsewhere. But he lives with this problem every day at work. He's getting ready to spend some serious money to solve his problem. So don't make the mistake of pretending that you know more about his problem than he does. You don't.

Even if you actually do know more about his problem than he does, you need to bury that deep down and not let it out. When it comes to the prospect's problem, you are the student and the prospect is the teacher. Give the podium to the prospect, and be a good attentive student.

That said, you know more about your solution than he does. You live with your solution every day. So don't let your prospect pretend that he's the only expert in the room. He isn't.

Hopefully you've seen customers with similar problems solve them with your solution. Unless your prospect has solved this same problem in a previous job elsewhere, it is probably his first time trying to solve the problem. But you likely have seen it before. A lot more times.

That experience is extremely valuable and should be appreciated by the prospect.

When it comes to your solution, you are the teacher and the prospect is the student. Time to swap places.

When you allow the prospect to educate you on his problem, and you respectfully take that information in and make valuable use of it, you are setting yourself up as a role model. Now when it is your turn to educate the prospect you have imprinted how that exchange should go just moments earlier. Do unto others, right?

Build something together

A competent techie (like you) could probably scan your solution's web site and understand what your solution does in just a few minutes. I'll bet that's what you did when you were originally interviewing for the job.

Your prospect has probably already done that too.

Being able to list your product's features, to drive a canned demo, to recite a scripted PowerPoint — these are all compulsory exercises for every SE. They don't differentiate you or help you win business.

And yet that's what we're asked to do every year in sales training. Practice the demo. Show how well you give the PowerPoint. [Sigh]

That stuff is neither interesting nor fun.

What is interesting and fun is helping your prospect connect the dots between problem A and feature B. Helping your prospect have that "aha" moment where she says "Oh, my life would be so much better if I just used your solution!"

To get to that moment, you and the prospect are going to have to mentally apply the solution to the problem together, and see if it really does what you hope. That's fun, that's creative.

You're going to have to approach it from the vantage of two experts coming at the question from different directions, working together to build something new.

There's nothing adversarial about it. There's nothing "sales-y" about it. It's two kids playing with Legos, building something new. In my humble opinion, it's the part of the job that makes it worth doing.

You can't feel rejected if you're the one saying "no"

"Get used to rejection — it's part of sales." That's a load of horse crap.

Nobody likes being rejected. Rejection sucks. I hate it. You should too. I'm not sure how telemarketers handle their jobs, being told "no" all day long every day.

If you do things the right way, you shouldn't ever feel rejected as an SE. Here's why: You're not putting on a Broadway show hoping the critics like it. You're having a reasoned conversation with a prospect about whether your solution is a good fit for their problem.

If your solution is NOT a good fit for the prospect's problem, you're not being rejected. You and the prospect are agreeing that your solution is not a good fit for the problem. That's not rejection. That's agreement.

When you say to yourself "I hope this prospect likes me" you're mistakenly thinking that it's about you. It's not. It's about the prospect's problem and your solution.

As an SE, if you find yourself feeling rejected after a meeting something went wrong with your approach further upstream. I'll wager that you weren't focused on the prospect's problem and determining if your solution was a fit. You probably just gave the presentation and demo and hoped they liked it. Replay the encounter in your head and see if that's it.

I'll go further and say that when you're worried about being rejected, the worst thing that could happen is that you're not rejected. When you're feeling like you might be rejected, it is an indication that you did something wrong earlier. If they go ahead and buy anyway, now you have no reason to spend the time figuring out what you did wrong earlier in the process. And so now you're likely to make the same mistake over and over again.

When you find yourself being afraid of rejection, it's your subconscious giving you a hint that you've gone out on a limb where you don't belong. You're not thinking about encounters with a prospect in the right frame of mind. Use that fear as a cattle prod to get your head right before you walk into your next meeting. If you're doing it right, fear of rejection shouldn't ever rear its head.

You can't help somebody with their baggage if you're carrying your own

When you meet with a prospect, the elephant in the room is the prospect's fear of the information asymmetry. There's not enough space in the room for another elephant.

Think about all the fears that could be going through the prospect's mind: What if this solution doesn't work as advertised? Will I not get my bonus? Will I miss that promotion? If this solution is a failure will I lose my job? Will other people lose their jobs? Will our competitors eat our lunch? Could we go out of business?

That's a lot of paranoia that could be going through a prospect's mind. The prospect needs to know that you are 100% focused on solving his problem so that he can feel comfortable making the decision to buy.

Your world, your needs, your desires do not belong in the room with the prospect. The only thing you should be focused on is the prospect's problem.

If you or your AE are behind quota and you "push" the prospect towards making a purchase he will naturally recoil away from your pushiness, and any credibility you might have had is gone.

If you are so insecure that you are afraid to deliver bad news to a prospect ("no, I'm sorry but our solution won't do that"), the prospect is going to sense that you are a "yes man" who will say whatever the prospect wants to hear, and your credibility will be shot.

If you have a need to show off and prove that you are the smartest person in the room, you will appear arrogant and the prospect won't want to hear what you have to say when you try to share information.

When you go to the doctor, does she tell you about her problems? Would you trust a surgeon if she told you she has a big mortgage and needs to do 10 surgeries per month to pay for it? Would you trust a doctor's recommendation to take a certain drug because he gets nice dinners from the pharmaceutical rep that sells the drug? Would you feel good about a meeting with a doctor if you spent time hearing about how her teenage son was getting into trouble at school?

You are the doctor. If you wouldn't want your doctor to do it in front of you, you don't want to do it in front your prospect. It is NEVER about you and it is NEVER about your AE. For the SE, it is always about the prospect.

Key takeaways

- Pay attention to the little things, because your prospect is

- Fight the urge to try to come across as the smartest person in the room

- Imagine that you are a coworker of the prospect and you are each experts trying to solve the problem together

- Make your job more fun by building something with your prospect

- You can't feel "rejected" if you and the prospect are agreeing that your solution isn't a good fit for the problem

- Whatever personal issues you might be dealing with, don't air them with the prospect

Just say no

Tick tock

Your most precious commodity as an SE is time — not money, but time. What you do with your time determines how much money you get back in return.

There is a clock that is always ticking. It's called "end of quarter" or "end of year." The buzzer sounds, and your company tallies the score, writes commission checks, and starts over. You can only meet with a certain number of prospects in a week. You can only take a limited number of trips in a month.

Just like money, you can spend your time, you can invest your time, and you can waste your time.

When you encounter a prospect, it takes a certain amount of time to determine whether the prospect is a qualified prospect. This is time you must spend as part of the normal course of doing business. (We'll cover how to do this later.)

If you've determined that the prospect is qualified, then additional time with that prospect is time invested.

If you determine that the prospect is not qualified — if you know that the prospect doesn't have a problem that your solution can solve — any additional time with that prospect is time wasted.

As an SE, you are closest to the information necessary to decide whether a prospect is qualified or not. You know better than anybody in your organization whether or not your solution is a fit for a prospect's problem.

If you wait for the AE to make that determination, it might come at the very end of the sales cycle. That's when you hear disappointing things from your AE such as "Oh well, we didn't win the RFP, but at least we tried." or "Wow, I had no idea they had such a small budget." If you're hearing these types of things, it means *you* screwed up much earlier in the process, when you had an opportunity to stop things from going any further.

Being thoughtful about how you choose to spend and invest your time is actually a job requirement. You help your company, your AE and yourself when you choose to avoid time-wasting activities, such as meeting for a second time with a prospect that isn't qualified.

When you shrug your shoulders and let other people commit you to time-wasting activities, the net result is no different than you pretending to be sick and playing video games all day.

If you are going to be as productive as possible in your role as an SE, you need to get really good at identifying and avoiding activities that are not going to yield results. You must be "lazy like a fox."

Understand that I am NOT suggesting that you become a workaholic.

Rather, I am suggesting that if you take a good hard look at all the things you are currently doing, 80% of them are likely a waste of time while 20% of them move the needle towards actual sales. I'd prefer to see you stop doing that wasted 80% of your day and do twice as much of the valuable 20%. In the process you'll get back 60% of your day to do whatever else you like.

To do this you must take the initiative with your AE and your manager to help make a determination of a prospect's likelihood of buying, and do it early in the process. If you do not do this, you are shirking your responsibility as a key member of the sales team. Worse, you are asking your AE and your manager to make an ill-informed decision. They will likely default to chasing the deal, and therefore continue to waste your time and their time on prospects that will probably not yield a deal.

Not everybody is a potential customer

Somewhere along the way somebody once said "everybody is a potential customer" and this became one of the pillars of sales. This is a time-wasting trap you must avoid.

The 83-year-old grandmother sitting next to you on the plane is NOT in the market for a cloud-based enterprise web content management solution.

Neither are 99% of the people who put their card in the fishbowl at the trade show hoping to win a free iPad.

Each lead is like a rock that needs to be turned over to see if there is anything valuable under it. If there is nothing under the rock, you need to move on to the next rock. The world is a big place full of lots of rocks.

The combined efforts of marketing, inside sales, and other departments in your organization are designed to help you weed out the bad rocks before they get to you, but they only go so far.

You and your AE need to get very good at quickly turning over rocks to see what is underneath them. The better you get at this exercise, the more successful you'll be in sales because you won't waste time with prospects that don't have a good chance of becoming customers.

Some rocks are easy to identify:

- You sell a solution that starts at $250,000 and the prospect says their budget is $5,000

- You work for HP and the prospect says her company only buys from IBM

- Your prospect says "we're really not looking for a solution to anything, I just wanted to do a survey of what's out there"

Most are harder to identify, and we'll discuss ways to do this a little later.

But either way the principle is the same: If you are wasting time with a prospect who is not going to become a customer, your competitor is investing time with that prospect you're trying to find who will become a customer.

Manage your time, or somebody else will waste it for you

As an SE, the three biggest threats to your time are, in order:

1. Your AEs

2. Your prospects

3. Everybody else in your company

AEs are single-mindedly focused on achieving THEIR quota. Not the company's quota, but their quota. AEs aren't typically paid on how well the company does, they are paid on how well they do. As a result, if you support four AEs, each of them has no problem if they try to capture 80% of your time, math be damned. If I was an AE, I'd do the same thing. It's selfish, but understandable. Ironically, you do want each of your AEs to be selfish and to do what's necessary for each of them to make their quota.

To add to the problem, AEs don't "pay" for your time. Since there is no meter running whereby AEs must carve out a portion of their pay to reimburse you for your time, you are effectively a free resource. They know that more of your time is a good thing for them. They may not know how to use it properly, but they know more of you is good for them.

Conversely, you probably support more than one AE, and you probably care about a larger quota than just one AE's quota. The difference in perspective can lead to conflicts between you and your AE. If you support two AEs, Tom and Sally, and they both have deals cooking, which one do you think Sally wants you to work on? And Tom, how do you think he feels about that?

We've all been in meetings where an AE makes commitments of your time to a prospect without checking with you first. "Yes Ms. Prospect, my SE would be happy to build a custom demo over the next few weeks for you and to come back and show you how wonderful our product is." And the prospect happily accepts. To a prospect, you're a free resource too. Of course the prospect is going to accept. It's no different than a prospect allowing an AE to pick up the tab from lunch.

So you get back to your hotel still fuming at your AE, and there's an email waiting for you from the corporate office. There's a big conference coming up, and they need you to work with marketing on a presentation that you'll have to give in two weeks at a trade show. Oh, and you'll be manning the booth for three days. And ding, another email comes in about an existing customer who's having problems with the solution and they need you to fly in for two days to hold their hand because support can't make them happy. What the...?

It happens over and over and over again.

If you don't manage your time, and learn how to say to your AE "I'm sorry but I don't think I have the bandwidth to get that done" you're going to be in a world of hurt. But when you do finally get your AE to understand how valuable your time is to a prospect, that will go a long way towards getting the AE to realize how valuable your time is to them as well.

Every day, with every request that comes in, you have a choice: Would you rather A) be at 60% of quota and get applauded for being a team player who works his ass off, or B) be at 150% at quota and be thought of as the guy who never has time to help out?

Pretty much everybody you encounter inside and outside your organization wants you to take option A, but the reality is that if you want to be good at your job and to enjoy it at the same time, you MUST try for option B. I'll go further and tell you that if you think option A is more attractive, being an SE might not be the right role for you.

The curse of the pipeline forecast

Disqualified prospects that remain in your AE's forecast are like a cancer that will slowly eat away at you and kill you.

Understand what happens with an AE's pipeline forecast. A lead comes in, gets assigned to them, and it's now in their forecast. Usually on a weekly basis your AE needs to get on a call with his manager to discuss the forecast.

AEs don't get a gold star for having a "clean" forecast. They get a gold star for having a forecast that makes senior management smile and say "looks like we're on target!"

It's the curse of information asymmetry, but applied to sales management. Senior management knows that the AEs hold all the cards. AEs know if a lead in their forecast is a gem or is a lemon, but they're not telling. It's not in their interest to tell.

So imagine an AE with 10 prospects, nine of which are worthless and one of which should be a home run for $2 million. Senior management must discount everything they get from AEs in their forecast. (Senior management is the buyer in the used-car lot.)

If the AE is honest and cleans up his forecast so he only has one prospect in it, listed at $2 million, his management is going to discount that (probably by about 50%) and say he only has $1 million in his pipeline.

So instead the AE leaves the other nine in there at some believable average number of $250,000 each. When they all get added up they total about $4 million, and after the 50% discount that management applies the AE's forecast is about $2 million, which is what he thought he was going to bring in to begin with.

Everything's great, right?

No, it's not. Because now you have nine prospects in the AE's pipeline that are utterly worthless. After a while your AE's boss is going to say to her "What's happening with these other nine? I see you haven't had any activity on them for a while?"

That's when you get the call from your AE saying "Ummmm, hey, we're going to have to spend some time with these other prospects. Can you block some time to do some demos?"

This is why you should aggressively try to disqualify the prospect as early as possible. You need to ask enough questions so that if the prospect isn't qualified you can go back to your manager and say "I asked X, Y and Z, and they said A, B and C. Clearly they aren't qualified so let's not waste time with them."

Even it continues to sit in the forecast, you need to look your AE in the eye and say "You and I both know that prospect isn't qualified. We're not going to waste time by doing unproductive things with that prospect — let's go invest our time in something that might make us some money."

Disqualify early and often

Operate from a paradigm of plenty. There are plenty of prospects out there, many with a real need for your solution. Work aggressively with your AEs to separate out the qualified from the unqualified prospects as early in the process as possible.

As mentioned earlier, at a minimum your prospect needs to have three things if she is going to become a customer:

1. She needs to have a real problem

2. She needs to know she has a real problem

3. She needs to be motivated to solve her problem

Don't assume because your AE asked you to get involved that these three items are checked off. Prospects meet with vendors all the time. They might be doing a survey of the market. They might be gathering information to use to force their current vendor to a lower price. They might just need to look busy for their boss.

But you, as the SE, need to confirm that all three of the above are checked before you move forward. Preferably in the first 30 minutes of talking to a prospect, ideally on the phone. Long before you consider getting on a plane to visit, you need to check for these three things. If you don't, shame on you.

Get very comfortable saying the following: "I don't want to waste your time, just like I don't want to waste my time. Do you mind if I ask you a few questions to see if it makes sense for us to be talking?"

As an SE, you might not think it is your job to disqualify prospects. Certainly your AE should be doing the same thing. But you've got the most time at risk if you go too far down the path with an unqualified prospect: RFPs where you're column fodder, custom POCs for prospects with no budget, and trips to a prospect's office where you meet with lower level employees who are simply gathering info for a market summary report.

It might seem counter-intuitive to you when I suggest that you go out and actively try to disqualify prospects. The more we sell the more we make, right? That's true, but it doesn't mean you should chase every prospect like they are the last one you'll ever meet.

If the prospect isn't qualified, you aren't going to sell anything to her. Time spent with an unqualified prospect is a waste of time and energy.

Get to "no" as quickly as possible

Traditional qualifying questions are not actually effective.

Questions like "What's your budget for this?" or "How many users do you plan to put on the system?" or "Can you make a three-year commitment up front?"

For real prospects, questions like these are threatening. There is already an information asymmetry that they are trying to address — but in the other direction. The last thing a qualified prospect wants to do is give the AE even more information. So qualified prospects hedge their answers, giving noncommittal, vague, and mushy answers.

Unqualified prospects don't really have answers to these questions. But they don't want you to walk out of the room. They are usually looking for free information, and if you shut them down then they won't get what they want. So they puff up their answers, usually giving noncommittal, vague, and mushy answers.

Hard to tell those two groups apart based on their answers, isn't it?

This is why we as SEs should actively try to get "no's" from a prospect using what are called "negative questions." Odd as it may sound to do this, what happens is that a qualified prospect isn't put on the defensive and instead actively tries to impress upon you how qualified they actually are, because they do in fact need a solution and they don't want you to dismiss them out of hand. Alternatively, unqualified prospects tend to agree with your "negative" statements and that lets you identify them right away and quickly move on to other prospects.

In practice, actively looking for "no's" sounds like this:

> You: "Since this is an enterprise solution designed for lots of users, it probably isn't a good fit for you since yours is such a small department."

> Qualified prospect: "Well actually we're evaluating it in our department with an eye towards enterprise deployment for everybody."
> Unqualified prospect: "That's probably true, but I'm still interested to hear about your solution."

> You: "Ours is a complicated system with lots of workflow capabilities, and you probably want something very simple."

> Qualified prospect: "Actually we've looked at other systems are they are too simple for our needs — we need complicated workflow capabilities."
> Unqualified prospect: "Simple would be good, sure. For my own reference though, tell me about your complicated solution."

The more you try to talk an unqualified prospect out of a deal, the more he'll let you. But the more you try to talk a qualified prospect out of a deal, the more the he won't allow it. He needs a solution, and he doesn't want you walking out the door without trying to help him.

So by looking for "no's" you actually tend to find the "yes's" much sooner.

Want a great fit, hate a bad fit

Just because your prospect has a problem and you have a solution doesn't mean that the two are a match. Your solution doesn't solve every problem. Since you're a technician, figuring out whether the two are a match shouldn't be hard for you.

AEs are optimists. They hear that a prospect has a problem and has money to try to fix it, and they'll happily try to sell their solution. They are the proverbial hammer salesmen to whom the entire world looks like a nail.

You're the technical person tasked with making sure the fit between your prospect's problem and your solution is a good one.

You and your AE should both be trying to disqualify prospects together. Your AE should focus on the commercial side of things. You should focus on the technical side of things. Technical stuff is the safe space you should feel good in. Dig in and ask the questions you need answers to, so you can understand the prospect's problem.

Most prospects are going to be much more comfortable answering your technical questions about the nature of their problem than they will answering your AE's question about their budget. There is a good chance the prospect won't answer financial questions until much later in the relationship. Until you've rebalanced the information asymmetry, your AE is going to have a great deal of trouble getting much information out of the prospect.

But if you take the lead early and focus on the prospect's problem, you'll see a different reaction. The prospect will be relieved, and it will show. They'll be grateful you want to understand them and their problem, and they'll share a ton of information with you. Pick your questions carefully, and in a very short amount of time you should be able to know from a technical standpoint whether you have a solution to their problem.

If you don't have a solution to their problem, now you've arrived where you need to be: you can say to your boss and your AE's boss "I asked X, Y, and Z, and they said A, B and C — we don't have what they're looking for." That's GOOD NEWS, not bad news. It means you can close the book on this prospect and spend your time elsewhere, where you might be able to make money.

Point the prospect in another direction if it makes sense

In evaluating a prospect, if you determine that your solution isn't going to solve their problem, but you have a sense of what might, the worst thing you can do is waste their time and your time trying to sell them something they don't need or want.

The best thing you can do is to TELL THEM you cannot solve their problem. Your prospect will be grateful for your candor, you will have a natural way of ending the meeting gracefully, and best of all your credibility as an SE will be through the roof with this prospect.

"But, but, but..." Your mind is revolting at the motion that this prospect is not going to buy anything from you today. Correct. You don't have a solution to their problem. Why would they? But the next time this prospect has a problem he needs to solve, you are going to have an open invitation to come back in and see if your solution would solve that different problem.

When you disqualify a prospect, you have an opportunity to plant seeds in the marketplace. Some grow into future sales where you plant them. Others catch wind and take root at other companies — maybe this prospect leaves this job and lands at another company, or maybe this prospect is friends with somebody who works at another company who has a problem that you can solve.

As an SE, when you encounter a prospect whom you cannot help, you want that prospect to walk away thinking "That SE was really helpful — She didn't waste my time and I'd talk to her again if I need help."

Help make your prospect successful, even if it means pointing them in another direction.

How to say goodbye

At the Oscar's when it's time for somebody to go, the orchestra starts to play. We don't get the luxury of those blatant cues.

You'll know when it's time to say goodbye. So get comfortable with saying some variation of the following when appropriate:

- "I'm sorry what we have isn't a good fit for the problem you're trying to solve."

- "I appreciate you taking the time to discuss your problem and our solution, and I'm sorry it wasn't a good fit. I wish you the best of luck solving your problem."

- "I'm glad we determined that our solution isn't a good fit early in the conversation so we didn't waste your time."

Not only will your prospect appreciate the candor, but your AE will be forced to remove the prospect from his forecast. Closure is good for the prospect and very, very good for you.

Key takeaways

- To an SE, time is money

- Most prospects you encounter aren't qualified and should be dismissed as quickly as possible

- Vigilantly guard against having your time wasted on phony prospects

- Sales forecasting methods set you up to have your time wasted

- Aggressively disqualifying early and often is your best protection against wasting time

- Try to get to a "no" quickly so you can find "yes" sooner

- Don't force your solution where it doesn't belong

- If your solution is not a good fit, be honest and tell the prospect

- When it's time to say goodbye, say goodbye

Your education

SOAP - not the kind you bathe with

SOAP is an acronym used by doctors to help them remember the most natural progression of how to work with a patient.

SOAP stands for:

- **S**ubjective

- **O**bjective

- **A**ssessment

- **P**lan

Let's walk through an example of SOAP in action. Imagine you go to the doctor for knee pain you're having. The doctor starts by asking you some questions: "What brought you here today?" "How long have you been experiencing this pain?" "Does it come and go, or is it steady-state?" These are subjective questions. She is probing what you know about the problem to better understand what might be happening. Channel this inquisitive doctor in your own questioning of a prospect. (SUBJECTIVE)

Then the doctor says "I think we should run some tests to get some more information: Maybe an x-ray and an MRI, and some blood work." She wants objective data. Hard facts. Most likely you don't have objective tests your company runs for a prospect, but you could ask if they've done some. "Have you assessed how much revenue you're losing because of this problem?" "Have you calculated how much time you're losing because of this problem?" "Have you measured how much money you're spending to deal with this problem each month?"

Channel the doctor again, looking for hard data.
(OBJECTIVE)

You might be anxious for an answer ("Another test?
More questions? Come on doc, what's wrong?") but the
doctor takes her time to get all the information she
needs to make an assessment. Only after the doctor has
gathered all the information she feels is necessary does
she move to an initial assessment. Finally, she says "I
think the problem is this... and here is why I think this."
You too should be very patient and not jump to
conclusions about the nature of your prospect's
problem. (ASSESSMENT)

After Subjective, Objective, and Assessment, it is time
for the plan. The doctor says "Here's the course of
treatment I recommend. We will solve your knee
problem, and here's how we'll do it." This is where your
presentation and demo come in. At the end. For the
same reason a doctor doesn't start a visit with an
explanation of how her surgery works, you shouldn't
start with your presentation and demo. Only at the end
will your presentation and demo be helpful to illustrate
how your solution can solve the prospect's problem.
(PLAN)

Ask yourself this: How would you feel about the doctor's
assessment and plan if she had skipped the part where
she asked you questions and gathered data about the
problem? Or how would you feel if you had walked into
that first visit and she had started with a PowerPoint
presentation about her education, experience and some
of the more famous patients she has, and had then gone
on to tell you about all the different treatments she
offers? Sound familiar to anything?

They teach this process to every student who goes
through medical school because it works. The doctor is

"selling" medical care. There is an informational asymmetry where the doctor knows more about medicine than you do. To "sell" you on treatment, she needs to learn about your problem and tailor a curriculum about your problem so she can educate you on the solution. That way you'll be comfortable enough to "buy" the solution.

I am not suggesting that you pretend to be an actual doctor or that you stick to this routine in some robotic manner. But there's no reason to reinvent the wheel. Every prospect has been to a doctor, and every prospect is familiar with the notion of being asked questions in order to diagnose their problem. For us SEs, the SOAP paradigm has been handed to us on a silver platter — it's very handy, easy to remember, battle-tested for years, and works with just about any conversation we might have with a prospect.

Seek first to understand

The less you understand about the prospect's problem the more you are just a walking advertisement, repeating your boilerplate message in the hopes that the prospect is tuned in enough to pick out the parts that resonate.

Using the previous example of a doctor's visit, imagine if you had knee problems and you visited an orthopedic surgeon and without spending the time to ask you about what's wrong he simply started telling you about the different surgeries he knows how to perform. How effective would that be?

And yet as SEs we regularly get introduced to a prospect by our AEs and right away pull out our PowerPoint and demo without thinking maybe this isn't the most effective way of doing things. The AEs are guilty too — they should know that this isn't an effective way of doing things but they encourage this all the time.

When the time eventually comes that it makes sense for us to present and demonstrate, the purpose is to eliminate the informational asymmetry we discussed earlier so that the prospect can feel comfortable making a decision to buy your solution. You cannot do that if you don't know what she needs to know.

If you want your prospect to care about what you are talking about, you need to know WHY she should care. You must take the time to ask her questions so that you can understand exactly what it is she is trying to do and why. With that knowledge, you can determine whether or not your solution is a fit for her problem. And if it is a fit, you can share the relevant information with her so that she will understand how the solution will solve her problem and will perceive the value in your solution.

If you're worried that the prospect doesn't want you to ask a bunch of questions, think back to the example about the orthopedic surgeon. Would you want the doctor to ask you questions? Of course you would. Not only does your prospect want you to ask questions, but the she expects it. If you skip this part, you've actually done something wrong in her mind.

So jump into the conversation early and simply say "Do you mind if I ask you a few questions?" And don't be surprised when you hear back "Yes — please." That's not only polite, it is genuine. She really does want you to ask questions.

If things are going well, asking questions might use up all the time in a first meeting. Great. If you run out of scheduled time and you're on the right track asking good questions one of two things is going to happen: 1) the prospect is either going to let the meeting run over or 2) she's going to ask you for another time to continue the conversation. Win-win.

There is no qualified prospect in the world who will turn away genuine, intelligent, thoughtful, assistance in trying to solve her problem if she doesn't have to pay for it. If a prospect does turn it away, she probably isn't qualified.

Purpose and Goal

When I meet a prospect, I make it a point to begin the conversation by establishing my purpose and goal of being part of the conversation. Usually something along the lines of "My purpose in coming here is to see if I might be of value to you. My goal is to figure that out as quickly as possible."

I don't just think that, I say it. I put it out there and make sure the prospect is A-OK with it.

"Purpose" is what's in it for the prospect. From a prospect's perspective, an SE's purpose should be "I'm here to see if I can help solve your problem." It is the WHY — why you are there, why the prospect should want to talk to you, why you could be of value to the prospect. It is what you are proposing to give to the prospect.

"Goal" is what you're after. From a prospect's perspective, an SE's goal should be "fulfill your purpose *as quickly as possible.*" It is the HOW — how you're going to interact, how you're going to try to help, and how the prospect will reward you for helping her. It is what you expect to get from the prospect in exchange for what you're proposing to give to the prospect.

You are here to try to help — that is your gift that you are giving away. In exchange, you expect the prospect to respect and value your time, just as you will respect and value her time.

By framing the conversation in this way, you get several very useful things:

- You've created an early warning alarm system. You cannot and should not move forward with the conversation if there is disagreement on your purpose and your goal. If the prospect has a problem with you wanting to know if you could be of value to them, and with you trying to figure that out as quickly as possible, you probably shouldn't be in the meeting. If you bump into that situation, ask the prospect what they think the purpose and goal of your involvement is. Odds are that when you hear it articulated you'll know for sure you shouldn't be in the meeting. Later you can ask your AE how the prospect got such a strange notion in her head.

- Your purpose gives you the very important permission to ask the questions to which you need answers. "I know these are sensitive questions, but as we agreed my purpose is to see if I might be of value to you and your organization. To accomplish that I need to ask some questions that you may be a little uncomfortable hearing."

- Your goal allows you to cut to the chase. You probably don't want to waste the prospect's time, and I know you don't want to waste yours. Your goal is not to spend two hours with a prospect and then hope to get another meeting. Your goal is to see if it is mutually beneficial for the two of you to even be talking. If it's NOT, better to know 5 minutes into the conversation than at the end of two hours.

- When the conversation goes down some rabbit hole that isn't a good use of your time, your purpose and goal are a great way to throw yourself a lifeline to climb out of the hole. "Ms. Prospect, I find all of this fascinating, but as we agreed my purpose in being here was to see if I could be of value to you. Is it ok if we bring the conversation back there?"

- It gives you a barometer to measure when the conversation is done. If the answer to "Could I be of value to you?" is NO, then it is time to politely thank the prospect for their time. Wish them the best of luck and get out of there. If the answer is YES, then it is time to discuss what the next step is and (not surprisingly) talk about the purpose and goal of the next meeting.

In the world of SE sales effectiveness, Purpose ("Can I be of value to the prospect?") is the rails that keep the train from going in the wrong direction and Goal ("Figure things out as quickly as possible") is the locomotive that keeps the train moving forward.

Listening

We learn when we listen. When we're talking, we're not learning. We might be doing something important when we are talking — like validating what we've learned or asking another question — but we're not learning when we're talking.

Listening is a skill you can and should practice. There are four general forms of listening, each a "higher" or "better" form than the previous:

- Passive - Essentially waiting for your turn to speak. We do this all the time automatically. "Any trouble finding our office today?" "No, no trouble at all." Mindless, effortless.

- Selective - Discussing a problem with a prospect but really only looking for an opening to pitch your product. "I read on your website that you have a SaaS option..." "Oh yes! We have SaaS blah blah blah..."

- Active - Listening carefully and reacting to the words said. "Does your system run on LINUX?" "Yes." Most SEs operate here. We're technicians. We're literal. It's how we think.

- Perceptive - You're hearing the words and listening, but you're also paying attention to what isn't being said, how things are being said, body language, what they might be thinking, why they are saying the things they are saying, and how they are acting. This is where we — both AEs and SEs — should operate. When AEs and SEs operate here you won't believe how many deals can be closed.

When we operate here we need to block our calendars for the annual Achiever's Club trip.

In my opinion the biggest determining factor for how much money you can make as an SE is how well you can listen to a qualified prospect. It is NOT how well you demo, how well you know your product, how well you dress, how well you fill out RFPs, or any of the other things you might do.

The more you operate with perceptive listening, the better an SE you will be and the more money you will make. Guaranteed.

Tactically, here are some thoughts and tips to help reinforce the need to listen more than you speak:

- If you or your AE is speaking, you are learning nothing about the prospect. The goal is to learn as much as you can about the prospect's problem. When you are speaking, you are not making money. Listen more = make more money. Same goes for your AE.

- "Verbal diarrhea" sounds unappealing. It is. Don't do it to a prospect.

- If your AE won't shut up, interrupt and get your prospect talking by asking questions. After the meeting (or better yet, BEFORE a meeting) agree on a hand signal that you can each use to tell the other to STOP TALKING.

- We have two ears and one mouth. Listening twice as much as you speak is a good rule of thumb. 80%/20% is better. 90%/10% is ideal.

- When it's your turn to speak, stop after you finish a sentence or two. Stop and wait. Unless the prospect facing you says something like "please go on", or "and?", or "tell me more", you're done. It's the prospect's turn to speak.

- Here's a helpful visualization technique. Imagine you have a microphone. When you speak, you're holding the microphone. Once you finish, you hand the microphone back to the prospect (this is a metaphor — don't hand an imaginary microphone back to the prospect — that would be weird). Now you wait. Don't take the microphone away from the prospect. The prospect speaks for as long as she wants. If you're listening perceptively, you'll know when you get handed the microphone back from the prospect. Now you speak again, but only when you are given the microphone. And by all means, give that microphone back to the prospect as quickly as you can. You don't want the microphone. Got it?

Getting permission

Fact: Nobody will ever get mad at you for doing what they just gave you permission to do.

So if the notion of asking the prospect a bunch of questions makes you feel awkward or nervous, ask for permission.

Example: Somebody in a restaurant comes over and grabs an empty chair at your table without asking. What a jerk. Same scenario but the guy first says "do you mind if I take this empty chair?" — now he's not a jerk because you said yes.

I get it — maybe the prospect is going to get defensive or angry if we ask questions. You're asking the prospect about why things are so messed up there, right? That could be a sensitive subject from the prospect's perspective.

If you ask for permission, 100% of the real prospects will say "yes, go right ahead." Any prospect that doesn't agree to let you ask questions isn't a real prospect. Get out as quick as you can. I don't care what odd-ball scenario you're dreaming up right now to prove that maybe some prospect won't let you ask questions. I promise you that oddball scenario isn't worth your time, which equals money.

Any prospect that won't let an SE ask questions to see if he can help solve the prospect's problem isn't a real prospect.

Getting permission is simple. It sounds something like this: "If I'm going to be able to help you, I need to ask some questions to better understand your problem, how it's affecting you and your organization, etc. Is that ok?"

It's not complicated, but it's very important.

Asking questions is not rocket science

When the time comes to ask questions, this is where things get easier, not harder.

You do not need to be an expert in the prospect's business when you walk in to talk about his problem. In fact, it is probably better if you are not, because if you walk in and try to act like you know the prospect's business, you'd be a poser. And the prospect will know it.

Reading a bunch of industry trade magazines to pick up the lingo for that sector and appear like you are somehow "in the know" is a waste of time. Save that energy for really concentrating on asking questions and listening to the answers.

The purpose of meeting with a prospect is for you to learn about his problem, and for you to educate him on your potential solution. If you go in thinking you already know all about the prospect, what you've done is basically pulled the pin on the ASSUME grenade and are now waiting for it to go off. Neither side should know what the other is going to say. If you did, what would be the point of meeting?

So how then do you go into a meeting with a prospect — perhaps with somebody very senior at the organization — and come across as thoughtful, intelligent, and generally somebody who they should spend some time and money with?

With simple questions like these:

- Would you mind telling me a bit about the problem you're trying to solve?

- Is that important? Why?

- Could we go over that last part again? It's not clear to me.

- Why is that a problem?

- Who is affected by this?

- What has kept you from solving this already?

That simple set of questions should get the prospect talking for 90% of the time and give you a wealth of information about the prospect and his problem. The intention is to give you an opportunity to listen and learn.

Once you get the ball rolling with one of these questions, you'll also have to master Jedi-like skills such as: nodding periodically, cocking an occasional eyebrow, and looking confused when you don't understand something. You'll have to learn how to say things like: "Please go on", "How so?", and "Tell me more about that."

This is not rocket science. It is easy. Don't let anybody scramble your head and tell you otherwise.

Empathy wins

The easiest way to really understand a prospect's problem is to try to put yourself in their position. Walk a mile in their shoes. Understand what their world looks like from their perspective, and you're on the way to understanding how you might be of value to them.

Empathy is not sympathy, although they are similar. Sympathy is listening to your prospect's problem and saying "that sounds like it sucks — sorry dude." Empathy is really getting inside the prospect's head and sharing the feelings of the prospect.

How do you do that? It's very simple — ask the prospect to help you.

"Mr. Prospect, it would really help me understand the problem you're trying to solve if you could let me see the world through your eyes when you encounter this problem. Could you talk me through some examples of this happening from your perspective?"

Once he gets started, role play as he talks. Imagine the scene as he is describing it. Ask questions where details seem missing in order for you to complete the picture. As you are imagining the story unfold, if you think he's going to turn left and he turns right, ask why. Probe as he tells the story. Really try to get into the situation.

When you do this, you're probably going to have a bunch of "really? I didn't know that" moments. Say that. Get clarity. Hopefully when you get to the end of the prospect's journey you'll have that "oh I get it now" moment, where you really understand and feel their problem. If you don't, go back because you missed something. As an SE you're looking for that "wow, that really sucks" feeling that bothers your prospect. When you feel that, you now know what they are trying to solve and why they are trying to solve it.

While it might sound silly to go through this exercise, there is an added benefit that comes from doing it. The prospect is now thinking "This SE is really listening — he really understands what we're trying to do here. He gets it."

As a bonus, your prospect is hopefully also thinking "And the SE from their competitor sure didn't do this — I don't think he really understands my problem as well as this guy does."

Curious George

Curiosity might have killed the cat, but to an SE it is an empowering life potion.

When you're in front of a prospect, it is essential to be yourself. Authenticity is critical if you are to establish rapport and trust with a prospect.

If you're like me, you're an SE because you like technology. As a kid you probably played with Legos, Erector Sets, Lincoln Logs, etc. (I might be dating myself here - sorry.) You probably took apart your toys to see how they work. You've done the same with technology I suspect.

So do it with the prospect's problem. Take it apart. Try to figure out what's broken. Maybe it's a people issue. Maybe it's a tech issue. Maybe it's a money issue. Who knows — go figure it out. It's a puzzle. Have fun with it.

If you're not a naturally curious little professor, try to channel one to help get into character.

Do NOT channel James Bond — slick, suave, debonair, knows everything. Your AE can try to channel James Bond if he wants. But you do not want to channel James Bond.

(Warning: I'm about to date myself in an even bigger way here) You want to channel Columbo, the old TV detective played by Peter Falk. You can find old episodes on YouTube. Watch a couple. He's always asking questions. He never stops with the questions. I think maybe every line of dialogue he ever had ended with a question mark. He has suspects, we have prospects. But he always got his suspects to talk. That's how he learned as a detective. Terrible haircut, nasty cigar, crumpled raincoat, rusted out old car. But always inquisitive, curious, wondering. That's a great role model for an SE (maybe not the cigar).

Remember something once said about scientific discoveries (Einstein said it, maybe?): most breakthroughs don't happen with a "Eureka," but rather with a "Hmmm, that's weird." Go have a breakthrough with a prospect.

Don't assume you're on the right track

Everybody has probably seen some variation of the comedy skit that highlights that when you ASSUME, you make an ASS out of U and ME. Right?

The Navy's version goes like this: "A little rudder early is better than a lot of rudder near the rocks."

As you dig into a prospect's problem, as you probe and ask questions, it is often the case that you can get lost in the weeds and end up going in the wrong direction. Take the time to periodically ask questions to make sure you're going down the correct path. You want to be focused on their problem and whether you can solve it. With all the information coming at you there might be a tendency to jump to conclusions or go down an unrelated rabbit hole.

As an example, I'll tell a story that once happened to me. I met with a prospect and the conversation went very well. I asked questions that identified a problem. I probed. I empathized. The back and forth was lively, engaged, animated. As we approached the end of our hour I said "so as I understand the problem you're trying to solve it is..." And the prospect said "Well yes, that is a problem but it's not why I asked you to come here today. That problem has no budget for a solution. I wanted to talk about..." Arghhh!!!

I had totally missed the chance much earlier in the conversation to verify that we were talking about the right things. Don't be an idiot like I was.

Key takeaways

- Use SOAP as a reminder of the progression for a discovery call

- Try to walk a mile in your prospect's shoes

- Take advantage of the good things that come from establishing your purpose and goal with the prospect

- Listening well is the difference between making ok money and great money

- As an SE, better to seek permission than forgiveness

- Use simple open-ended questions to get your prospect talking

- Improve your understanding of the prospect's problem by getting into character

- Really pick apart your prospect's problem so you can understand it better

- Check early and often to make sure you don't get lost in the weeds

The prospect's education

Bringing it all together

You've listened, you've learned. You've been patiently asking questions and letting the prospect educate you. Now it's time to address the information asymmetry we've talked about.

This may seem complicated but it isn't. Here's a true story from a while back showing how simple the entire process can be:

I was an SE working the East Coast, and at the last minute I got asked to cover a meeting in Texas for another SE who had come down with the flu. With no choice in the matter, I hopped a plane the next day for Dallas. No opportunity for any sort of discovery whatsoever. Such is the life of an SE sometimes.

We walk in to the meeting, the AE does the intros, and then she popped open her laptop to do her usual 20 minute "who we are" introductory PowerPoint. You know the one: when we were founded, employee headcount, top customers, key partners, etc. [Sigh]

The prospect stopped the AE and said "I don't mean to be rude, but we really want to cut to the chase. We've looked at all your competitors, and none of them do what we really need done. We just want to know if you can do what we need, and if so you'll get the deal." [Sounded to me like permission to ask questions]

My AE actually wanted to continue with her PowerPoint, but I reached over and plugged my laptop into the projector and asked "What exactly are you trying to do, and why?" [Time to get an education from the prospect]

The prospect: "Our entire marketing plan is dependent on capturing [XYZ] data from our website visitors and reporting it back in an [ABC] format" [Couldn't get more concise than that]

Me: "Oh, do you mean capturing data like this (I show the screen) and getting back a report like this (I show the report)?" [A single-feature, one-minute demo]

The prospect: "Perfect! That's exactly what we need — when can you get us paperwork to sign?"

Meeting over in about 5 minutes.

It can be this easy. Not often, but it does happen. While short, this example highlights the foundational principle of being an SE: Your prospect must make his own decision of whether to buy or not to buy, and that decision will largely be determined by the information you choose to give him. Give him the right information in the right manner and this can be an easy process.

Teaching sells

It may sound like hyperbole, but neither you nor your AE are in the business of selling anything. You are in the business of empowering people to make a buying decision. A sale will occur when a prospect has gathered enough information to satisfy her concerns about deciding to buy your solution.

As Jeffrey Gitomer — author of best-sellers like *The Sales Bible* and *The Little Red Book of Selling* — likes to say, "People don't like to be sold, but they love to buy."

Home Depot offers courses on do-it-yourself techniques for home renovation, and product flies off their shelves. Famous chefs do TV shows about how to cook their favorite recipes, and their cookbooks become best sellers. Golf club manufacturers sponsor clinics on hitting longer drives and their clubs sell more.

It is all about helping a prospect cross that threshold from "I don't know enough to make an informed decision" to "Oh this makes sense to me. I can this decision."

You — the SE — are in the business of balancing that information asymmetry so the prospect can cross that threshold. You are the Obi Wan Kenobi that says to Luke you too can learn the Force and go defeat the Empire.

When you empower a prospect with the right information, you build the prospect's confidence so she can overcome the fear that prevents her from buying.

As techies, we are inclined to think that the more technical trivia we can unload on a prospect, the better.

That is flat-out wrong. The art of teaching is knowing just what small bit of information the student needs to know to have an "aha" moment. Chain a few of those "aha" moments together and your prospect will suddenly feel like Luke in light saber training, blocking zaps while blinded by the helmet with the blast shield down.

It's safe to say that if Obi Wan Kenobi had delivered a two-hour presentation and demonstration of all the features of the Force, Luke (and the audience) would have been yawning and Star Wars would have been a one-and-done screen flop.

Think about that the next time you get ready to give a generic 27 slide PowerPoint presentation, followed by an exhaustive demo of every feature in your solution. If you've dug into a prospect's problem, hopefully instead you can create a handful of "floating zapper while wearing a blast shield helmet" moments that will have the prospect going "Whoa, I can do this..."

And if YOU think it's fun to give a five-minute demo that knocks the prospect off her feet, believe me when I tell you that your prospect will love it even more.

Don't bury the lead

What's everybody's favorite topic of conversation? Themselves.

Why would you think your prospect is any different?

This is why a statement such as "ours is a multi-tenant cloud-based solution" doesn't really resonate with a prospect. But a statement like "I understand you needed a solution yesterday, and the good news is that ours is a multi-tenant cloud-based solution so you could be using it tomorrow" rings like a bell. Because you've led with why they should care about the info you're about to give them.

Here's a handy exercise that won't take as long as you think it will. Fold a piece of paper in half vertically. On the right-hand side (not the left) write down each of the key features of your solution. When you're done, over on the left-hand side write down the answer to the following for each feature: "So what? Why should a prospect care?"

Now look at your list and learn to use it by starting on the left — "So what? Why should you care?" and then moving to the right — what the feature is. When you're having a conversation about features and functionality, or giving a demo, introduce each point by answering the question "So what? Why should the prospect care?"

So for example, if on the right you wrote "SaaS solution," on the left you might write "We handle all the hassle associated with installation, maintenance and subsequent upgrades." So in this example, instead of simply saying "Ours is a SaaS solution," you would instead start on the left and say "We remove all the hassle usually associated with installation, maintenance and upgrades, since we're a SaaS solution."

The reason the "why should I care" portion is on the left is because we need to lead with the "reason why the prospect should care."

If you reverse the order, it becomes "Ours is a SaaS solution, which is important for you because it means we take all the hassle out of installation, maintenance and upgrades." There's a good chance that she wasn't really listening until you got to the "why she should care part," and she'll either ask you to repeat the first part ("it's a SaaS solution") or worse she'll be too polite to admit that she wasn't listening and she'll let you go on, not knowing what you said originally.

Deciding to buy is usually a private affair

It shouldn't come as a surprise, but you and your AE probably won't be in the room when the decision to buy actually occurs. Despite all the hype you hear in various sales training programs about the need to "climb the ladder" in order to get to the decision maker at your prospect's organization, these days that decision maker is usually high up enough on the ladder that she doesn't want to or have to spend ANY time with a vendor's sales team.

If you labor under the delusion that your standard presentation and demonstration is actually the thing that makes a sale happen, then for you it's true that you need to try to eventually trap the ultimate decision maker in the room so you can re-run your infomercial. Looking back on your experience though, do the facts really line up to support this delusion?

In my experience, you must approach that first meeting from the perspective that the prospect you are meeting with is in fact the decision maker. Because she is, in one very important respect.

When the meeting is over, she is going to make the decision of whether the things she has learned from you are worth sharing. And if she does, then she is going to have conversations about what she has learned. From you with others

You won't be in the room when she does share that information.

Pause and let that sink in. The critical next step in the prospect's journey towards making a buying decision will happen when you and your AE will NOT be in the room with the prospect.

Your prospect is going to meet with her boss, her team, or her colleagues, and she is going to be asked "hey you met with that company — what did you think?" Your prospect is not going to have your PowerPoint or your demo handy. The only thing she is going to have is whatever she has remembered from all the information you've given her. She is going to have to make a strong argument in your favor if the process is going to move forward towards a sale.

This is why you — the SE — drive the sales process. You're the teacher. You're the one who diagnoses the prospect's problem and educates her on how and why your solution will solve her problem. When you meet with the prospect, you are training her to be an evangelist for your solution within her organization. Make her look good in front of her peers, and you've almost got the sale.

People remember stories

When SEs are first hired into an organization, the first thing they should learn are the good stories. The bits and bytes and other techno-stuff you'll pick up as you go along. But if you want to be useful out of the gate, you need to know out of the gate the good success stories of how your solution has helped customers.

And then when the sales teams get pulled into periodic training meetings, the SEs should be given a hall-pass so they can go into a separate room where they meet with a group of people representing customer support, marketing, services and product management. And the topic of the conversation should be "Recent successes where our solution was such a good fit that our customers rave about us." I want the stuff that I can brag about when my parents say "so what's so special about this stuff you're selling?"

That would be pure gold for an SE.

Cinderella, Goldilocks, The Three Little Pigs and Little Red Riding Hood. How long has it been since you've heard those stories? I'll bet you could tell the basic version of each right now if you had to.

Our brains are wired for stories. Long before written language, people remembered things via orally related stories. Our ancient ancestors did not pass along knowledge and wisdom via bulleted PowerPoint slides or technical specification sheets. They told, and remembered, stories.

Now think back to your last internal meeting where the speaker ran through a PowerPoint deck. How much of that can you remember? Can you remember any of it? A single bullet point maybe?

Your prospect is no different. A week after you've left her office, when she bumps into a colleague who says "how'd that meeting with the vendor go?", you'd better hope she remembers something from the meeting.

The way for that to happen is to tell a good story. So rather than saying "our solution can decrease your costs by 14%," tell the quick story about how another customer used your solution to decrease their costs by 14% and saved a ton of money, etc. Make it concrete. Bring it to life. That way they can pass along that knowledge and wisdom to the next person they meet with.

Case studies might be an ok starting point, but they're usually written in "corporate speak." If you're going to use material from case studies, you should tell the story in your own voice. You must bring the story to life. Little Red Riding Hood wouldn't work as well as it does if it was reviewed and edited by your company's legal department. Same rule applies when you use material you found in a case study. Try to give it some late-night camp-fire pizazz.

Pattern matching

Not just any story, mind you. The story must resonate. If your prospect's problem is all about increasing revenue, you can't tell a story about cutting costs.

The stories you learn need to be filed away and drawn from at appropriate times to be useful when you're in front of a prospect. They really should be categorized by business value. Things like "increased revenue," "cost costs," "reduced complexity," "improved quality," or "improved user experience." These are the "themes" of your story, in the same way that love, redemption, fear, and heroism are themes for novels.

When you pick a story to tell, your theme should match the theme of the problem the prospect is trying to solve.

So let's imagine that your prospect's problem is that they're a large consumer products company with many brands, and they have a lot of marketing people creating and curating digital content. It's total chaos — no good collaboration tools, no workflow tools, no version control, etc. Essentially, they need to reduce complexity. That's the theme.

Assuming your solution handles this, it's ok if you don't have any experience with a large consumer products company. All you need to have is a story to tell about a customer in another vertical with the same theme — reducing complexity. Maybe you've got a customer in the banking sector who had the same type of challenges. That story should work, because similar problems were solved with your solution.

Going further, perhaps the person you're talking to is a VP of marketing. But the story you heard was told from the perspective of the head of IT at the other customer. Change the narrative voice. Tell the story about the banking customer from the perspective of a VP of marketing at that company.

It's the same problem and the same solution. By changing the "hero" of the story to one that your prospect will identify with, you help the prospect to internalize the story and make it her own.

Depending on the nature of your solution, there are probably anywhere from 3-7 business themes that your solution addresses. I'd suggest that as an SE, you should try to learn at least one, and up to three stories for each business theme that your solution addresses.

Don't make a big project out of this exercise. An encyclopedic catalog of stories is only marginally better than 8-10. Just make sure the 8-10 you know are very good ones.

Answering questions is not rocket science either

The secret to being good at answering questions is simply to be good at listening to the question being asked.

Earlier in my career I sat on the other side of the table as a prospect, buying lots of technology solutions. Before that, I had already spent time in my career as an SE, so I was judgmental of the SEs I met with. I played a secret game where I used to mentally grade them using this scoring system for each question I asked:

* Listening to the question and making sure it is understood (asking clarifying questions is allowed) - 50%

* Answering the question that was actually asked, not something else - 50%

* No deductions for having to get back to me after the meeting (so long as you do actually close the loop later)

* No deductions if your answer is not what I wanted to hear (it might affect my view of the solution, but not of the SE)

A dismally large percentage of SEs couldn't get a passing grade (60%). Some got almost zero points.

The few who were able to score 100 points — which by my estimation isn't hard, just uncommon — received most of my orders.

It goes back to the different levels of listening. Even if you're not operating at the ideal "perceptive listening" level, you ought to be able to hear a complete sentence, process it, and give back an answer that addresses the question asked.

Here are some real examples where the SE thought he knew the answer already and stopped listening to the rest of the question:

Q: "Speaking of browser support *[SE stops listening]*, our corporate IT policy has us locked into an older version of IE, version 9. Do you support it?"

A: "Oh, we work with IE, Firefox and Chrome."

Q: "I realize that tuning a large database can be hard *[SE stops listening]* — will our DB folks have enough information in the tools and documentation to get things configured optimally once we're up and running in production?"

A: "Our professional services folks would be happy to give you an SOW to help you tune your database."

Q: "Let's say I'm a non-techie type of person working in marketing *[SE stops listening]*, but I've been asked to do double-duty as an administrator of this solution — will I find it too complex to figure out without a strong techie background?"

A: "Oh, we have lots of features designed for marketers."

Saying "no" builds credibility

Picture this: You're meeting with a prospect and at the point where she is asking you questions about features and functionality. Can it do this? Yes. Can it do that? Yes. What about that other thing? Yes! Yes, yes, yes, YES! Total love-fest. Meeting is going fantastic.

Then she says "Oh, can it also do this?" She has just hit the boundary of your solution. You know that saying "no" might ruin the mojo, bringing it to a screeching halt. What to do?

Fudge it? Say "Sure, with a little tweaking" and hope they don't ask to see it? Promise that it's coming in a new version? Bad moves.

Just say "Sorry, but no — it doesn't do that."

One of two things happens, and they are both positive:

1) The very unlikely scenario is that you've just qualified OUT of the deal. I say unlikely because if it was a deal breaker it probably would have come up sooner and you wouldn't have been in a love-fest. But if you did just disqualify out, congratulations you are now free to spend your time with a prospect whose problem you can solve and not waste time with somebody whose problems are not a fit for your solution. Your only post-mortem question you need to ask yourself is whether you could have elicited that outcome sooner and saved yourself some time.

2) The much more likely scenario is you just bought a boatload of credibility. When you walk out of one of those love-fest meetings where the answer is yes-yes-yes-yes-yes, your prospect is going to have a moment a

little later when she thinks "Hmmm, I wonder if that SE was feeding me a line of BS. Nothing is that perfect." But that little "No" gives her the ability to tell herself "He wasn't afraid of telling me what I didn't want to hear — he said 'no' to one of my desired features." That little "no" made all the other "yes's" that much more credible, a critical factor for your prospect to address her fear of choosing your solution.

So don't be afraid when you must say "no" — be glad for the opportunity. Either way you win for saying it.

Never Answer a Question that Wasn't Asked

Nine times out of ten, it can only get you in trouble.

We've all done it. Here's one I goofed on recently: "Does your product work with Chrome and Firefox?" "Yes, absolutely." I should have stopped there. But for some reason I can't explain, I felt compelled to say "...but Safari we have problems with." Why? I dunno. It seemed like a good thing to say. It was true. But they hadn't asked, so it wasn't relevant.

What happened? Somebody in the room who wasn't a decision maker, who wasn't really paying attention, and who really had no interest in what we were talking about, piped in and said "Oh, that might be a problem with some of Tom's people in marketing — I think they might be on Macs."

I so mad at myself. I totally derailed the momentum, and now we were talking about something tangential. All the mojo we had 60 seconds earlier was lost. All because I answered a question that wasn't asked.

Shame on me.

Any time you feel like taking the conversation somewhere the prospect didn't ask it go, just stay on the rails.

Key takeaways

- Don't overcomplicate this – your prospect may only need to know one or two things

- Teaching sells, because what you're doing is correcting the information asymmetry

- Always lead with the business value before the tech info if you want to keep the prospect's interest

- By teaching the prospect, you prepare her to sell your solution later on when you're not in the room

- Use stories because they are so memorable

- Pick the right stories so they resonate with the problem the prospect wants to solve

- Make sure that you really understand the question being asked before trying to answer

- Saying "no" doesn't disappoint a prospect, it builds trust

- Don't volunteer information that wasn't asked for – it cannot help you

Presentations and demos

Let's test the null hypothesis

ASSUMPTION:

Giving a Powerpoint Presentation and a demonstration is a highly effective way to impress somebody early in a relationship and to determine if it makes sense to continue having further discussions.

TEST:

We'll take a group of adults who considered themselves "single," and ask each of them to develop a PowerPoint presentation about them self, along with some sort of demonstration of their skill or competency or some other trait they feel is compelling.

Then we'll ask them to use their PowerPoint presentations and demonstrations whenever they go out on a first date with somebody they've met, and ask them to record the effectiveness of the material.

How do you think that experiment will turn out?

Visual aids

During SE conversations with a prospect, the only legitimate reason to break out a PowerPoint deck is because either 1) you need to use a slide in lieu of drawing a diagram on an ink board, or 2) your demo system is down and you need to use screen shots to mimic a demo walk-through.

I say "during conversations with a prospect" meaning every interaction with a prospect until you reach the point late in the sales cycle where you are presenting to an audience, and plan to do a theater-style presentation and demonstration. Everything prior to that is a two-way conversation. Breaking out a PowerPoint deck does not facilitate two-way conversations.

Similarly, your demo system is just a visual aid to be used sparingly during a conversation with a prospect. You should leverage it to highlight or validate a point you've just made in conversation. You should never make it the center of attention and turn yourself into a tour guide, showing every little bell and whistle of the system.

For example, you never want to find yourself saying "ok, now let me take the next 30 minutes to run through all the features." If that comes out of your mouth you should give your AE permission to kick you under the table.

Rather, when you find yourself saying something like "our solution will save you a lot of time and cut down on a lot of errors by giving you a simple, intuitive user interface to capture the data you are looking for," you can punctuate that by saying "let me quickly show you the screen I'm talking about so you have a sense for what I mean." Once you show that screen, you continue the conversation and ignore the demo system until you need to showcase another point you've just made.

When you use the demo system to validate a point you made in conversation, you build credibility with the prospect. As you continue the conversation and your credibility grows, you can start to skip the visual validation of the points you're making, until you get to the point that you are explaining the key solution benefits and related features without having to demo anything.

This is the nirvana you're seeking as an SE. If the prospect isn't looking for validation in the form of a demonstration, it means you've become the trusted advisor. It means you're addressing the information asymmetry for the prospect, and helping the prospect to become comfortable with making a buying decision.

Which is why "less is more" when it comes to presentations and demonstration.

Infomercials

When we're asked to give "the standard presentation and demo" for a prospect, what we're really being asked to do is to give an infomercial. As I understand it, the economics of infomercials is that you show them to hundreds of thousands of people in the hope that hundreds of people will buy.

Makes sense, but not to me if I'm the one giving the infomercial to one person at a time.

Seems to me that if my company really wants to operate like this my company should bring one of us SEs into a studio with professional video production capabilities and let us record the presentation and the demo once, edit it to make it perfect, and then just give the video to the AEs to show. Then they wouldn't need so many SEs, and the remaining few could just take calls from the prospect who have questions after watching the video.

And yet every year we're herded into a room at the annual training meeting and we're asked to showcase how well we give the stock presentation and demo. What's the point?

Sadly, every seasoned SE I've ever worked with simply shrugs and says "Don't sweat it. Just stumble through it so they can check the box and then we'll go back to doing what we actually do in the field."

It's this mindset that causes AEs to falsely believe that we're "demo dollies," whose sole purpose is to come in, do the PowerPoint and demo, answer a few questions, and then wait in the wings hoping we get a chance to do a POC or an RFP.

This is all wrong.

If we are going to do a full-blown presentation and demonstration, it should be the last thing we do in the sales cycle. It should be done in the "validation" phase where we've already convinced the decision maker that our solution will solve her problem, and now we're coming in for a meeting with a much larger group (*i.e.,* an audience) so that she can get buy-in from all the stakeholders in one go. And our presentation and demo is anything but canned — it must be completely tailored to the prospect's problem and how we'll solve it.

That's when we should be "presenting and demo'ing," not any time before.

Presentation tactics

When you do have to give a presentation and demo, there are several things you should do as you prepare in order to help you make that presentation as effective as possible:

- Use the following for your working title: "Our understanding of your problem and how we'll solve it for you." Every slide in your deck and every feature you're going to show MUST speak to that title. If it doesn't, toss it. Keeping the audience's attention is THE secret to making a good presentation. Making sure you are ALWAYS talking about how you're going to solve the prospect's problem is the only way to consistently keep the audience's attention. Imagine somebody in the audience asking "so what" every time you make a point. If you don't have an answer to "so what?", you shouldn't be making that point.

- The moment you put up a slide, if the audience is paying any attention to you they will start reading it. Guaranteed. While they are reading the slide, they aren't listening to you. Also guaranteed. People can either listen to something being said or they can read — they cannot do both at the same time. Good presenters know this and wait for the audience to finish reading. If you think you're going to have to wait an awkwardly long time for everybody to finish reading the slide, that's a clue that perhaps you have too much information on the slide.

- If your slide contains everything you plan to say, and you are simply going to read (or paraphrase) your slides to the audience, I promise you that by the third or fourth slide nobody will be listening to you because you're only telling them what they just read. Better to eliminate all the bullets from your slide and simply leave the slide title as a visual placeholder for your audience. Now they must listen to you.

- Nobody likes dimmed rooms and PowerPoint presentations unless they just ate a big lunch and want to snooze. The phrase "Death by PowerPoint" always gets a chuckle because it's so true. I don't care how charismatic you are, you will never hold an audience through a 27-slide deck that lasts an hour. Boil down your presentation to the critical essence for your prospect. The audience will only remember three to four things max from your deck. The less "noise" you give them, the better the chance that they'll remember the things you want them to.

- Guy Kawasaki, Apple's legendary evangelist for the Mac, has a simple 10-20-30 rule for any PowerPoint presentation: maximum 10 slides, maximum 20 minutes long, and minimum 30-point font size on all slides. If you're thinking that you'll never be able to fit all your bullets onto a slide with a 30-point font, you're right. That's why he has the rule.

- Garr Reynolds has built on Guy Kawasaki's rule and written a book called *Presentation Zen*. As an SE, it is a "must read." It gives great examples of how to use PowerPoint as a visual aid to help you tell your story, and is a quick enough read that you can finish it on a short flight. I can't recommend it enough.

If you watch a bunch of TED talks, you'll see that most of the presenters incorporate the above guidelines into their presentations. It's not an accident — these techniques work. And most of them can be learned and used by you in your everyday work with less effort than you're putting in today.

Key takeaways

- If PowerPoint and demos are so effective, why don't we use them in things that really matter?

- PowerPoint and demos are only visual aids to help you validate or substantiate points

- Infomercials are only useful at the very end of a sales cycle when you know exactly what the audience wants to hear

- When you do have to present, take advantage of the techniques that have been proven effective

Conclusion

I've tried to articulate in these pages things that have been there sitting staring at us all along. For a long time I I didn't see them because they were hiding in plain sight. Now that I do see them I cannot NOT see them.

Prospects buying complicated technology solutions are George Akerlof's prototypical used-car buyer. Without an SE, your AE is seen as just another used-car salesman, with the prospect worried about buying a lemon. Information asymmetry dominates the situation.

As an SE, you are the one positioned to address that imbalance and thus to drive sales.

When I think about the SEs I admire, they do intuitively all of the things I've written about, and they do them well. Ask them to articulate why they do it that way, and they often just shrug and say "because it works."

I didn't invent any of the things on these pages. I just tried to assemble them into one (hopefully not too long) book because I think that they can all be learned. And I think that the starting point for learning how to do them is to understand why you should do them. Start with the "why," and the "how" just flows naturally.

I'm hoping that now you can replay interactions you've had with prospects and "see it" too. See why some things worked. See why some things didn't. See how it could have been done differently.

I suspect that the sales training we must all endure each year will continue to be some mish-mash of "let's practice the new PowerPoint deck and let's practice the demo and then call it a day." Pity.

We can do it better. Everything here can be taught, and you don't need special skills or talent to learn any of it:

- Don't waste time with unqualified prospects

- Determine if your solution is a good fit for a prospect's problem

- Empower the prospect with the relevant information so she can feel comfortable making a decision to buy

Sales doesn't have to be a zero-sum game. If every prospect out there is discounting our solutions by 50% because they think we're selling lemons, we could all double our quota if we just got better at really convincing them of the value of our solutions. If we don't all get better, I don't mind running circles around my competitors who refuse to learn their craft.

If you have any interest in continuing the dialog, I'd be delighted to hear from you. I really do see this book as an open source contribution to the SE community. If you've got ideas on how to make it better or more useful, I'm all ears.

John Haldi
me@johnhaldi.com

A Note on Sources

It is fair to say that there are many things to be found in this book which are ideas that have already been put forth by others. I would go further and say that pretty much any idea of value found in these pages was born elsewhere.

Candidly, I'm an avid reader and over the years I've read probably over 200 books focused on sales, sales training, business, psychology, etc. With hind-sight I wish I'd kept copious notes and detailed information on where I'd learned things along the way. But I didn't. Shame on me.

In writing this book I realized that what I've done is simply to assemble in one place all of this good stuff that I've read or been told along the way. It would be apt to use the phrase "I'm just standing on the shoulders of giants."

I would very much like to be able to annotate the book and provide detailed footnotes identifying each of my sources any time I used something from them. I fear if I did so I would never be 100% complete, and then I'd appear to claim as my own something I wasn't able to properly footnote.

Let me therefore please state unequivocally and for the record that if you read something in these pages and you think "that's pretty smart", I do NOT deserve the credit. Somebody else came up with that idea and if you were to ask me via email I'd try my best to provide you with where I first heard/saw it. Of course, if you find anything in these pages to which you think "that's idiotic", I'll take full credit for that.

Acknowledgements

I could never have written this book without the input and encouragement of a some very special people. I'd like to take a moment to thank them all. (And if I've left anybody off, please please please accept my humble apologies – it wasn't intentional.)

The seeds for this book were planted a few years ago at dinner with Tom Brown (my manager at the time) as he patiently let me ramble on and on about my opinions on what's wrong with the way SEs are taught their craft. When I finally ran out of steam he hoisted me on my own petard, so to speak, and said "great, can you put all that together as a presentation when we're all together for our meetings in Texas next week?"

If Tom put the noose around my neck, Jeremy Anderson (a coworker) pulled the lever to drop the floor from under me when he left the presentation and told me I ought to write all that stuff down in a book. Naturally I blew him off, but then he called me a few weeks later and told me he had just landed a new job using all the things we had covered in the presentation, and that I really had to write it all down for other people to use. (Tom was none too pleased that Jeremy left, if you're curious. And I'm not sure Tom knew this little vignette prior to my putting it here.) Without Tom and Jeremy's support and encouragement this book never would have gotten started.

My wife Kristina Song has been a constant source of support throughout the entire process. Always one to stay positive, she continued to smile and encourage me even after reading draft upon draft that showcased that I am decidedly NOT a good writer. Even when the drafts were truly terrible, she was kind enough to find positive things to say like "it's definitely your voice!"

I'd like to acknowledge Erik Hartog as my personal superhero. Despite English being a second language to his native gibberish, Erik was instrumental in editing the overall content of the book. (Erik suggested that I say this in the acknowledgements, fully expecting me to NOT say it. But one of the great joys of self-publishing is that nobody stands between the author and the Kindle store.)

Alan Schwarz (if he sees this) will probably cringe that his name is associated with the book, considering how amateurish my writing is. But he provided critical insight into helping me frame the intended audience and tone of the book. If a better written version ever gets created, it'll be because he takes the time to rewrite the thing for me.

My friend Sander Biehn was also instrumental in providing encouragement and leading by example. It's always easier to follow in somebody else's footsteps.

Another great friend, Rich Sanders, also provided critical counsel and motivation along the way.

Preston Chin also deserves a shout out for patiently reading early drafts of this book, even though he had much more important things to do with his time. His enthusiasm for the project was just what the doctor ordered when I was losing momentum.

And finally, special mention must be made of Martin Query, to whom this book is dedicated. Martin is the AE extraordinaire who took me on many years ago as a completely green SE and taught me the right way to do things, and also vigilantly kept me from learning all the bad habits that management tried to teach us SEs. There's no better teacher or salesperson out there. When I told him I intended to write down all the things I'd learned from him he – in typical fashion – said "what on earth for?" He's probably right, but I did it anyway. And I'm not worried about embarrassing him since he'll probably never read this. Why would he? There's nothing in here he doesn't know already.

What's With the Title?

As a techie you may already be familiar with Ruby on Rails, a web application framework created by David Heinemeier Hansson in 2004.

Ruby on Rails is opinionated, meaning that the authors acknowledge that theirs is one of many ways to accomplish something but the authors believe it is the best way to do it. It attempts to provide a framework that automates or eliminates the drudgery of common tasks associated with web application development, freeing the developers to focus their time on the fun, creative, problem-solving aspects of development. I think it would be fair to say that Ruby on Rails helps developers to be "lazy like a fox". And finally, Ruby on Rails is open-source, which means that it gets better through the input of the developers who use it.

This book derives its inspiration, hence its title, from Ruby on Rails. It too is opinionated, in that there are other ways to reach the same outcome but I believe it is the best way to do it. It too is an attempt to provide a framework that automates and eliminates the drudgery of common tasks associated with being an SE, hopefully freeing the SE to spend more time on the fun, creative, problem-solving aspects of sales. It too encourages SEs to be "lazy like a fox". And finally, I'm hoping that this book begins a much-needed open discussion in the SE (and larger sales) community about the critical role that SEs play in the sales process.

Made in United States
North Haven, CT
21 September 2022

24411575R00082